# IRELAND'S
# COAST

CARSTEN KRIEGER is a professional photographer based in the west of Ireland. His unique images are highly acclaimed and over the past decade he has become one of Ireland's foremost photographers.

Conservation plays an important role in his work. He has worked as a staff photographer for the *IPCC* (*Irish Peatland Conservation Council*), was the picture editor and photographer for the environmental magazine *Rocky Road*, he is a regular contributor to *Irish Wildlife* magazine and is currently representing Ireland at the international *Meet Your Neighbours* project.

Carsten has published five books on Ireland's landscape and wildlife, including *Ireland: Glorious Landscapes*.

## Dedication

I would like to dedicate this book to all conservation workers in Ireland who dedicate their time and strength to a noble cause and to the Irish fishermen who endure a hard and undervalued job.

Although it seems at times these two groups are working against each other in the end their goal is the same: keeping Ireland's coast the breathtaking place it is, teeming with life and beauty.

As always this is for Ina, Jonah and Lucy.

# IRELAND'S
# COAST

## CARSTEN KRIEGER

THE O'BRIEN PRESS
DUBLIN

# Contents

# FOREWORD

Half-a-billion years ago Ireland was otherwise and elsewhere. The sub-equatorial supercontinent that contained Ireland was washed by a great sea, the shore of which can still be detected, not around, but through the middle of Ireland. Since then the drag and pull of continental drift and tectonics has shifted and sundered our little landmass.

Repeated glacial grooming and bathing in fluctuating seas have rendered it the familiar 'shaggy dog-on-its-side' of today.

The seas continue their influential work – aggressively so on the Atlantic coast, more benignly to the east. Our coast is also soothed by the warm Gulf Stream and nourished by the cold upwellings in the Celtic sea.

The amazing scenic variety that typifies our coastline may be viewed as a grand collusion of art and science: of relentless elemental sculpting on obdurate geology. This work in progress has multiple expressions in the headlands and islands, inlets and estuaries, dunes and beaches … that define our country's margin.

The twice-daily tidal rhythm of exposure and concealment imposes a lifestyle of tolerance on the flora and fauna. The zonation of intertidal seaweeds and winkles reflects this. In the hidden world of deeper water, molluscs, crustaceans and fish respond to other ecological imperatives. At the top of the food chain sea birds and marine mammals exploit this fecundity.

In summer our coasts become nurseries for mind-boggling assemblages of fulmars, kittiwakes, guillemots and razorbills, jostling for footholds on cliffs and rocky islets. These seabird cities are among the greatest nature spectacles in Europe.

The first people to come to our shores were drawn to river outfalls where shellfish could be gathered and migrating fish hunted. The arrival of agriculture did little to deter fisherfolk from occupying the coast, building permanent settlements and constructing boats fit for purpose. Trading added a further consolidating dimension leading to the development of ports. Such coastal foci have, down the ages, acted as conduits of cultural infusion.

Today coastal utility is in transition. Solid traditional industries, fishing and shipbuilding, have been overtaken by more speculative enterprises like fish-farming. Increasing energy demand proposes offshore windfarms and less intrusive wave-harnessing. Much recreational activity is also now associated with our shores. Eco tourism has become a significant consideration in the revitalisation of our coastal communities: we are nevertheless only beginning to evaluate and appreciate our birds and whales and breath-taking coastal scenery.

Carsten Krieger's marvellous photographs remind us of what we still have and warn us about what we have to lose.

*Gordon D'Arcy*

# INTRODUCTION

My first memory of Ireland's coast are the smooth pebbles at Ross Behy Strand at high tide, the incoming surf and that unique clacking sound that comes with each retreating wave. This was the first time I laid eyes on the Atlantic Ocean and it was probably the time my love affair with the coast began.

The coast, the magical border between land and sea, the dividing line between earth and water, calls out to all of us. It's a place of constant change that seems to hold the memories of our own ancestral beginnings.

Ireland, this small island at the edge of Europe, calls some 7,500 kilometres of shoreline its own. Ireland's coast as we know it today is a product of the latest glaciation during the ice age. Around twenty thousand years ago most of Northern Europe, including Ireland, was covered by a huge ice sheet. The sea level was some 120 metres lower than today, and Ireland and Britain were joined together and had a connection to the European mainland.

When temperatures started to rise about fifteen million years ago the glaciers eventually started to melt and water levels began to rise. It was then that the retreating ice carved the landscape, leaving behind the sea loughs of Ireland's northern coast, the great peninsulas of the southwest and many other features of today's coast like the drumlin islands of Clew Bay.

The rising temperatures also allowed plants to get a foothold and they were soon followed by animals that crossed the quickly disappearing land bridge between Britain and Ireland. Following the animals were the first humans who arrived in Ireland around ten thousand years ago. It is thought that these hunters and gatherers arrived in Northern Ireland by boat from Scotland, other groups probably managed to cross the land bridge from southern Britain into southern Ireland before it got swallowed by the Irish Sea.

At this time Ireland was covered by an almost impenetrable boreal forest and the first settlers stayed mainly along the coast and river estuaries. Evidence for their presence can still be found today in forms of heaps of shells above the high tide line. Imagine a group of people on a sheltered part of a beach, sitting around a fire, roasting and cooking their cockles, razor clams and mussels. When the meal is finished they just toss the empty shells behind them. Over time these midden heaps reached considerable height and today allow archeologists a unique insight in the diet of our ancestors. Today these heaps are covered by sand and grown over by dunes and other vegetation, but from time to time wind and tides uncover pockets of shells, often at the base of shifting dunes, and allow even us non-archaeologists a glimpse in to the past.

Over the following centuries Ireland and its coast changed dramatically. The climate became warmer and more humid and sea levels rose fur-

**Above**: *Machair, Silver Strand, County Mayo*

ther. The hunter-gatherers settled down, became farmers and started to cut down trees to make space for fields. The combination of climate change and human interference meant the end of the forests and the rise of the bogs. Evidence of this process can still be found today and some of the most impressive examples are located at the coast. Rinevella Bay at the Shannon Estuary holds an example of what is known as a drowned or petrified forest; the middle and lower shore of this bay is made of peat with countless tree trunks still embedded in it. Once a dense forest must have covered what is now the estuary of Ireland's longest river, deer and boar must have roamed where today seals and dolphins are swimming. Places like this are mind boggling and encourage us to look into our distant past.

Today Ireland's coast is a jigsaw of many different habitats: sandy beaches, including adjoining dune systems and the unique 'machair' – a sandy grassland that can only be found in the North West of Ireland and the west of Scotland – make up more than two thousand kilometers of the Irish coast; river estuaries provide shelter for salt marshes and vast mudflat areas; there are also rocky shores are made of rock platforms, pebbles, stones or boulders, soft cliffs made of stones and dirt and hard cliffs that rise to a height of several hundred metres.

Although people over time ventured and settled inland the coast remained a vital and constant influence on the Irish people. Dune grasses provided the raw material to thatch houses, seaweed became a common fertilizer, but first and foremost the sea and coast have always been a source of food. In more recent times, seafood has grown into an important industry.

Being a fishermen on an island sounds like the perfect job. Unfortunately cheap fish imports from overseas, over fishing and resulting regulations and quotas make life anything but easy for Irish fishermen, especially for the smaller local enterprises. But there are still many thriving ports around Ireland like Howth, Dingle or Killybegs whose fishermen not only supply for the domestic market but also export their goods around the world.

For many people, however, the coast means one thing: holidays! The Irish coast is probably the most important asset for the tourism industry and is marketed to suit both the active and not so active visitor. Water sports like sailing, surfing and kayaking have become very popular. More recently the tourism industry has also discovered the coastal wildlife and eco tour operators are now offering dolphin, whale, seal and other wildlife watching trips.

This however puts the coast and its inhabitants under constantly-growing pressure. Littering, pollution, over-fishing and destruction of habitat are just a few factors that threaten Ireland's coast.

Making this book was a journey of discovery in many different ways. First there was the actual journey around the fringes of Ireland by car, boat or on foot. At times, this journey seemed to go on forever, on narrow country roads around long stretched peninsulas, along the shores of sea loughs and over choppy seas to some mystical island.

It was also a very personal journey. In the early stages my goal was to capture the wild and varied

*Below : Fulmars, Loop Head, County Clare*

**Right**: Beadlet Anemone

landscape of the Irish coast. But soon it became clear that the Irish coast has more to offer and I went back to my roots as a wildlife photographer trying to capture the coastal fauna from the nervous hermit crab to the mighty fin whale.

Although we like to think of the coast as a wild place, it has been very much shaped by human hands. It's impossible to travel along the coast without seeing piers, harbours, lighthouses and watchtowers; most of the time this built landscape is rather picturesque and forms an integral part of Ireland's coast. It's only another small step from photographing coastal architecture to photographing its creators, carving a living out of the coast's resources or simply enjoying it.

The wild coast, the built coast and all its inhabitant are all part of a tightly-woven net and once I embraced the idea of capturing all aspects of Ireland's coast I found myself in, for me, rather unusual circumstances. I visited a sail maker on the Mizen Peninsula, followed the building of a traditional sailing boat in West Clare and photographed the

**Right**: Hermit Crab

surfing championships in Bundoran. I spent many hours onboard a boat on the Shannon Estuary trying to get the perfect dolphin shot, I was photographing fishmongers in Howth and lost myself in the eerie intestines of Hook Lighthouse. But taking this plunge into the unknown not only made me meet some fascinating people, it also changed my perception of my art and in the process made me a better photographer, I hope.

The goal for this book was to show all aspects of Ireland's coast but unfortunately there is only so much space and no book of this size can do total justice to the wealth of subject matter. So in the end this is a personal view and I hope you enjoy looking at it as much as I enjoyed making it. Or as my countryman Heinrich Böll put it in his book *Irish Journal*:

*'Es gibt dieses Irland: Wer aber hinfährt und es nicht findet, hat keine Ersatzansprüche an den Autor'* ('This Ireland exists: However if you go there and can't find it, the author will not be responsible for compensation').

**Above**: *The Saltees from St Patrick's Bridge, County Wexford*

# THE SOUTH EAST

The counties of Wexford and Waterford occupy the southeast corner of Ireland, an area also known as the sunny southeast. Statistically this part of Ireland enjoys more sunshine than the rest of the country, a very welcome fact for the outdoor photographer.

The far southeastern corner of Wexford is more or less one endless stretch of beach, starting at Wexford Bay on the eastern coast and ending at Ballyteige Bay in the south. Wexford Harbour at the Slaney Estuary is almost entirely surrounded by sandbanks that only leave a small opening between Raven Point in the north and Rosslare Point in the south. The Wexford Slobs, an area of reclaimed land known as polders, and the natural estuarine

habitats of Wexford Harbour are a very important wintering place for wildfowl. Each year around 20,000 birds spend the winter season here. Photographing wildlife in Ireland in winter calls for luck with the weather and the light, and unfortunately my visits always coincided with grey and wet winter weather.

Further south lays another haven for birds: The Saltees. These rocky islands host Ireland's second largest gannet colony and are a breeding ground for several other bird species, like puffins, guillemots, fulmars and razorbills, and for grey seals.

West of the Saltee Islands the Hook Peninsula stretches out into the Celtic Sea and marks a change in the coastal landscape. Rocky shores grow into

**Right**: *Spined Sea Scorpion*

**Above**: *Fisherwoman at Wexford Harbour, County Wexford*
**Opposite**: *Kilmore Quay Harbour, County Wexford*

sheer cliffs that open up into secluded bays protected by protruding headlands and sea stacks: Waterford's Copper Coast.

Exploring Ireland's south east coast takes some effort. Although the coast runs in quite a straight line, the narrow country roads – which are especially picturesque in early summer when the banks are covered in pink flowers known as thrift – endlessly twist and turn before they reach the sea. I lost my way more than once and equally often I wasn't sure if I had reached the destination I had in mind. But in the end this didn't matter. I found enough subject matter to fill several books and the sunny southeast lived up to its name many times.

Situated around five kilometres off the south Wexford coast and built on bedrock laid down two- to six-hundred million years ago, the Saltee Islands are one of Ireland's natural wonders. The name given to the Great Saltee and its companion Little Saltee is probably of Norse origin, '*salt-øy*', meaning 'salt island'. A visit to the Great Saltee in windy weather when salt spray quickly encrusts anything will reveal the reason for the name.

The Great Saltee is privately owned by the Neale family. The late Michael the First made a vow as a ten-year-old that one day he would own the Great Saltee. In 1943 he realised his dream and in 1956 he was crowned the first prince of the Saltees. In reality however the island belongs to the birds: the elusive Manx shearwater, razorbill, guillemot, kittiwake, gannet, puffin, cormorant and other species occupy every inch of the island during spring and summer. In autumn more than 100 grey seals also come to the island to breed. Unless you suffer from ornithophobia or have been watching Hitchcock's *The Birds* recently a visit to the island is an amazing experience.

***Above***: *Birds of the Great Saltee:* **Left**: *Gannet.* **Right**: *Puffin*
***Opposite***: **Top left**: *Razorbill.* **Bottom left**: *Cormorant chicks.* **Right**: *Cormorant*

'All people young and old, are welcome to come, see and enjoy the Islands, and leave them as they found them for the unborn generations to come see and enjoy.'

*Michael the First*

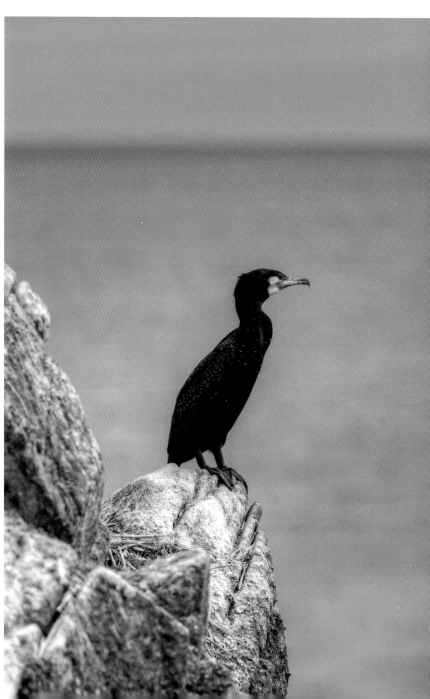

**Below** : *Booley Bay, Hook Peninsula, County Wexford*

**Above**: *Hook Head Coast with Saltee islands in the distance, County Wexford*

**Above**: *Hook Lighthouse, County Wexford*

The Hook Lighthouse is not only one of Ireland's best known landmarks situated in beautiful surroundings, it is also one of the world's oldest working lighthouses, and Ireland's earliest established lighthouse.

The origins of Hook Lighthouse date back to the 5th century AD when St Dubhan, a Welsh monk, established the first beacon on Hook Head. St Dubhan, whose name is the Irish for 'fishing hook', had founded a monastery nearby and soon became aware of the dangers that the waters around Hook Head held for sailors. The first beacon wasn't much more than a fire built on top of a pile of stones but it provided a crucial guiding light for vessels entering Waterford Harbour.

The first proper lighthouse was built in 1172 by Raymond LeGros, a Norman nobleman, who also used the tower to guard the entrance to the harbour and protect his land from invasion. LeGros however never saw the building finished and entrusted it to the local monks of the priory of St. Augustine before his death. Hook Lighthouse was eventually finished in the thirteenth century by William Marshall, the Earl of Pembrokeshire, and the monks continued to man the tower until 1641 when civil war broke out and they were forced to abandon the lighthouse.

It took twenty years and numerous shipwrecks to re-establish Hook Lighthouse, but in 1667 the light started to shine again and has done so ever since. In 1996 the light became automated and only five years later Hook lighthouse opened its doors to visitors and has become a major tourist attraction since.

A structure as old as Hook Lighthouse is unsurprisingly surrounded by numerous legends and stories. Various lighthouse keepers have reported the noise of footsteps during the night and one man even claimed to have seen the ghosts of the monks who had presided over the tower in the past.

Other stories claim that gold brought to Ireland by the Knights Templar is hidden in some secret room or within the walls of Hook Lighthouse.

**Above**: Herons and dusk, Bannow Estuary, County Wexford

*Below* : Blackhall Strand, County Wexford

***Opposite****: Tramore Harbour Lighthouse, County Waterford*
***Above****: The Castle, Ram Head, County Waterford*

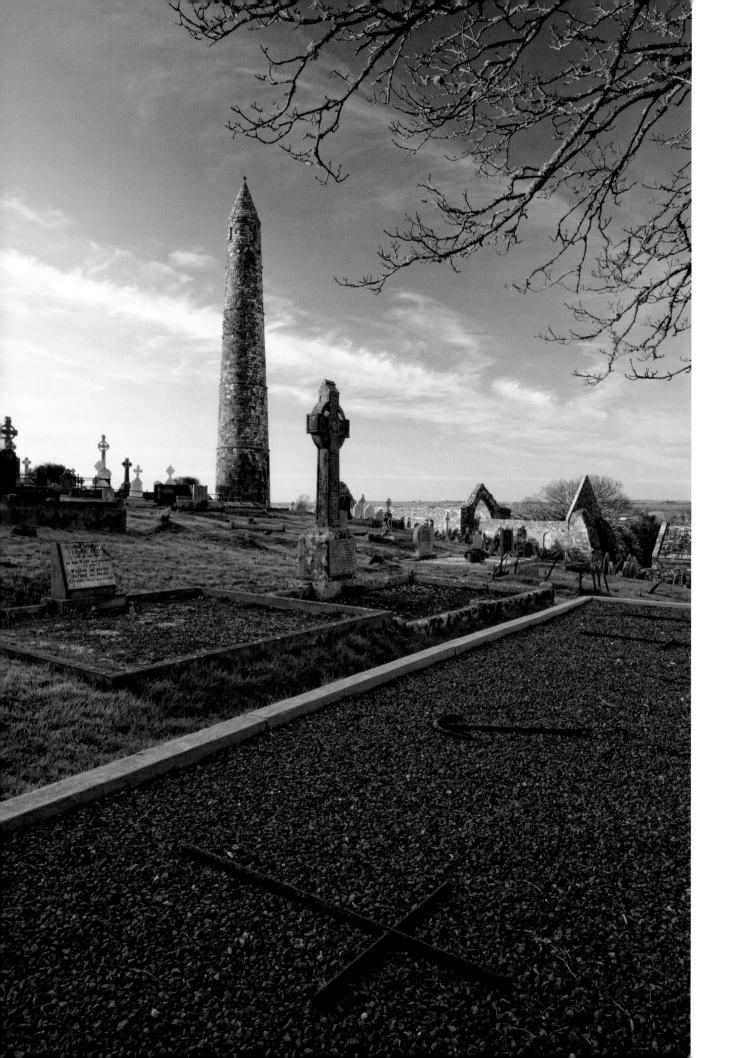

Ardmore is well known for its church and twelfth-century round tower. In a corner of the graveyard that surrounds both, a plain patch of gravel can be found, only decorated by some simple metal crosses and an anchor. Known as the Sailors' Grave, this resting place holds the remains of the twelve crew-members of the S.S. *Ary*.

On 8 February 1947, the S.S. *Ary* left Port Talbot in South Wales with a crew of fifteen and a cargo of coal destined for Waterford Harbour. The winter of 1947 was one of the coldest and harshest on record in the UK and Ireland. Biting east-erly gales and unprecedented snowfall held Western Europe in its grip for weeks. In these conditions the S.S. *Ary* set sail. Only a few hours into the journey the already bad weather worsened. The high seas caused the cargo to shift, destabilizing the vessel. All countermeasures taken by the crew were in vain and some-time after nightfall the order to abandon ship was given. All crewmen made it safely into the lifeboats before the S.S. *Ary* sank. During that cold and stormy February night onboard the lifeboats, all but one man died from exposure.

On Wednesday 12 February Jan Dorucki made his way up the north-ern side of Ardmore Bay. He was the only survivor. Later he recalled finding his crewmates frozen to death after the first night in the boat. Becoming nervous and afraid he decided to push the corpses into the sea. That Jan survived three days of sub-zero temperatures and stormy seas in a small lifeboat on the open water is nothing short of a wonder.

Over the following days the dead bodies of twelve sailors were washed ashore. They were buried together on the 18 Feb-ruary at Ardmore cemetery. The other two sailors have never been found.

**Opposite**: *Sailors' Grave and Roundtower, Ardmore, County Waterford*
**Above**: *Montagu's Blenny*

***Opposite and above***: *Ballyvooney Cove, Copper Coast, County Waterford*

The Copper Coast makes up the major part of the Waterford coast and stretches from Tramore to Dungarvan. Dramatic cliffs and sheltered coves with sandy beaches make this one of Ireland's most picturesque locations.

The Copper Coast, a designated European Geopark, gets its name from the nineteenth-century copper mines, remains of which can be found all along the coast. The Copper Coast can best be described as on outdoor geology museum that allows us to look back on 460 million years of earth's history. Volcanic eruptions, ancient deserts, deep river valleys and immense glaciers all left their mark in the cliffs of the Copper Coast.

**Above**: *Coumeenoole Bay and Great Blasket, County Kerry*

# THE SOUTH WEST

Ireland's southwest is caressed by the warm waters of the Gulf Stream and also receives a lot of water from above in the form of mist, drizzle, rain and various other forms of precipitation. The resulting mild and moist climate turns the counties Cork and Kerry into a natural garden with a plant life unlike anywhere else. Lush woodlands that seem to have come right from the Mediterranean cover valleys, hillsides and expand right down to the seashore.

The Cork coastline starts at Youghal and meanders in and out forming tiny bays, inlets, coves and harbours that are punctuated by headlands and promontories.

North of Baltimore these promontories grow bigger and become more defined. Mizen, Sheep's Head, Beara, Iveragh and Dingle are the great peninsulas of the southwest reaching out into the Atlantic Ocean like fingers. These peninsulas are divided by long stretched bays: Dunmanus Bay, Bantry Bay, Kenmare River and Dingle Bay are former river valleys that became flooded when the glacial ice sheets of the last ice age melted.

The Dingle Peninsula, once described, as 'the most beautiful place on earth' by *National Geographic Traveler*, and the Iveragh Peninsula, better known as 'The Ring of Kerry', have become major tourist attractions; the coastal drives around these promontories are world famous and during the summer months it is often stop and go on the narrow roads.

The other peninsulas are less overrun by visitors, but equally pleasing to the eye. Sandy beaches and sheer cliffs are dramatically backdropped by the spectacular mountain ranges that form the backbones of every single of the peninsulas. A book on West Cork published some years ago is entitled *A Place Near Heaven* and I couldn't think of any phrase more appropriate to describe the southwest.

***Above****: Castle Haven, Castletownsend, County Cork .*

**Below** : *Storm and Lighthouse, Galley Head, County Cork*

*Below*: Toehead Bay, County Cork

*Opposite*: **Bottom left**: Fish farm, Kenmare River, County Kerry. **Top left**: Fishing nets, Coolmain Bay, County Cork. **Top right**: Fish, Dingle Harbour, County Kerry. **Bottom right**: Trawler, Dingle Harbour, County Kerry

Lough Hyne is a saltwater lake located in the very southwestern corner of County Cork. It is a truly unique place seemingly insulated from the world by the surrounding hills and forests that provide shelter from all but the most severe winds. The lake is connected to the Atlantic Ocean only by a narrow tidal channel known as 'The Rapids' that provides the water exchange between the lake and open sea. This makes Lough Hyne essentially a giant rock pool with a rich flora and fauna. The lake has been studied extensively since the 1930s and was declared Ireland's first marine nature reserve in 1981.

I know a lake where the cool waves break

And softly fall on the silver sand

And no steps intrude on that solitude

And no voice, save mine, disturbs the strand.

*(from 'Lough Ine' by Fitz-James O'Brien 1828-1862)*

**Opposite top**: *Lough Hyne, County Cork*

**Opposite bottom**: *Black Sea Urchin*

**Above**: *Union Hall Harbour, County Cork*

In the summer of 1631 Baltimore fell victim to what is thought to have been the worst ever pirate attack in Ireland. Earlier that year two ships under the command of a renegade Dutchman known as Morat Rais the Younger had left Algiers. Before reaching the Irish coast they had already seized several smaller vessels and killed or imprisoned their crews.

In the early hours of that fateful summer morning more than two hundred corsairs landed in the cove, burning houses and carrying off with its inhabitants. More than a hundred men, women and children had been taken and most of them never heard of again. The most likely scenario is that they ended up at the North African slave markets and spent the rest of their days as galley slaves or concubines in the harems.

The beacon overlooking the entrance to Baltimore Harbour was erected in 1849 as a warning sign to seafarers and is a notable landmark in the area. The more than fifteen-metre high structure is also known as 'Lot's Wife' or 'Pillar of Salt' for obvious reasons.

Across the narrow channel lies Sherkin Island, one of the many islands of Roaringwater Bay (the most beautifully-named bay in the whole of Ireland in my opinion), with its lighthouse that marks the other side of the narrow entry to Baltimore Harbour.

*Opposite top*: Baltimore Harbour, County Cork
*Opposite bottom*: Seven-Armed Starfish
*Below*: Baltimore Beacon and Sherkin Island, County Cork

*Below* : *Fin whale and common dolphin off the Kerry Coast*

***Above****: Barley Cove, Mizen Peninsula, County Cork*

**Above**: *Dawn at Schull Harbour, Mizen Peninsula, County Cork*

Just outside the village of Goleen on the Mizen peninsula Christophe Houdaille has set up his workshop in a most unusual location; Christophe is a sail maker and he runs his business out of a deconsecrated church. Needless to say I was thrilled when Christophe allowed me to visit him and his team. Photographing a craftsman in such a unique setting is something special.

Christophe is one of only a handful of traditional sail makers in Ireland. After learning his craft and sailing around the world for eight years he settled in Ireland and established his own business, Fastnet Sails, in 2003.

While chatting away about regattas, boats and his work I also learned that Christophe had been assigned to make the sails for the *Seol Sionna* boat building project I was documenting in County Clare. A typical Irish coincidence!

***Below*** : *Christophe Houdaille of Fastnet Sails, Goleen, County Cork*

**Above**: *Mizen Head Bridge, County Cork*
**Opposite**: *Sheep's Head Lighthouse, County Cork*

Mizen Head Lighthouse stands on a rocky outcrop connected to the mainland by a reinforced concrete suspension bridge. The original bridge, the first of its kind in Ireland, was built in 1909 to allow the lighthouse keepers easy access to their workplace. After the lighthouse was automated in 1993 Mizen Head was transformed into a visitor center and the bridge became one of the major attractions.

After a hundred years of service, however, the extreme weather and environmental conditions had taken their toll on this landmark building. The new bridge, pictured here shortly after completion, opened to the public in 2011. It is an exact replica of the old structure the only difference being the deck, which is now seventy centimetres wider.

The rocky ledge runs far into the sea,

and on its outer point, some miles away,

the lighthouse lifts its massive masonry,

A pillar of fire by night, of cloud by day.


And as the evening darkens, lo! how bright,

through the deep purple of the twilight air,

Beams forth the sudden radiance of its light,

with strange, unearthly splendor in the glare!

*(from 'The Lighthouse' by Henry Wadsworth Longfellow 1807-1882)*

*Above*: Ballydonegan Strand, Beara Peninsula, County Cork
*Opposite*: Pallas Harbour, Beara Peninsula, County Cork

The Beara Peninsula with its rugged coastline and carved mountain ranges is still a well-kept secret even after its northerly neighbours Iveragh and Dingle have been overrun by mass tourism for decades. This is both surprising and welcome especially if you take into account the fact that Beara more than rivals its neighbours not only in scenic beauty but also in a rich built heritage.

For a photographer Beara is a treasure chest and the only problem is the abundance of subject matter ... and the weather. Due to its topography Beara creates its own microclimate and the official weather forecast is practically worthless. One half of the peninsula can be bathed in sunshine while the other half, only a short drive over the mountains, is being drenched.

**Opposite**: *Loughaunacreen, Beara Peninsula, County Kerry*
**Above**: *Garinish Strand, Beara Peninsula, County Cork*

*Below* : Bantry Bay, County Cork

**Above**: *Fog over Bantry Harbour, County Cork*

*Above*: *Illauncrone, Iveragh Peninsula, County Kerry*

*Opposite*: ***Bottom left***: *Leaves and seaweed, County Kerry.* ***Top left***: *Sea milkwort, County Kerry.* ***Top right***: *Seaweed and jellyfish, County Cork.*

***Bottom right***: *Sea carrot, County Cork*

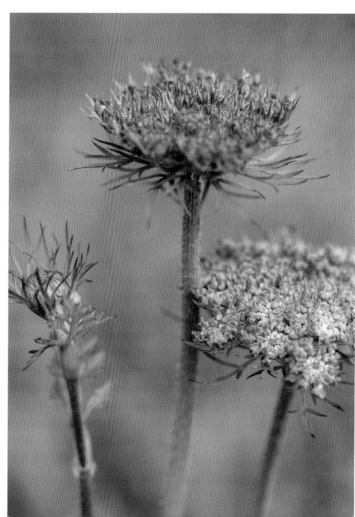

**Below** : *Blackwater Estuary, Iveragh Peninsula, County Kerry*

**Above**: *Derrynane Quay, Iveragh Peninsula, County Kerry*

I don't consider myself to be a spiritual person but there are places where even I envisage the possibility of a greater entity, a global spirit or whatever you may call it.

Skellig Michael is one of those places. This towering sea crag and its brother, Little Skellig, sit some twelve kilometres off the Kerry coast. Skellig Michael raises cathedral like to a height of over two hundred metres, Little Skellig reaches around 130 metres. Even from the mainland the shape of these rocks has considerable impact, they almost look like crowns rising out of the water, and make it clear there is something special about the place.

My first trip to Skellig Michael on a fine spring day coincided with perfect conditions. A calm sea (a rather rare event around the Skelligs), light winds and soft light filtered by clouds.

To reach the top of the island an almost vertical climb is necessary, following some six hundred steps that were built into the rock face sometime around the year 588 AD. For someone carrying several kilograms of photo equipment and suffering from vertigo this is not an easy trip. But the sheer spirit of the place makes it all worthwhile. Putting this 'spirit of the place' in words is something I have tried many times, but always failed. Words like 'tranquil', 'mighty', 'beautiful', 'mysterious' come to mind, but do nothing more than scratch the surface.

It is a place where it is easy to feel close to a greater power and not surprisingly Skellig Michael was home to a monastery for almost six hundred years between the sixth and thirteenth century AD. The buildings of this monastery still exist today and are in astonishingly good shape considering the power of the elements around the Skelligs. The six beehive huts, two boat-shaped oratories and a medieval church together with several stone crosses, slabs and graves make it easy to imagine early monastic life on this lonely outpost.

To call this life hard would be an understatement. The lack of wood or turf would have made heating and cooking difficult to. There was fresh water and just enough soil to run a small vegetable garden. During spring and summer there were birds and eggs but in autumn and winter this food source disappeared and even fishing must have often been impossible due to the regular occurring violent storms. But maybe bodily comfort becomes of less importance in a place like this.

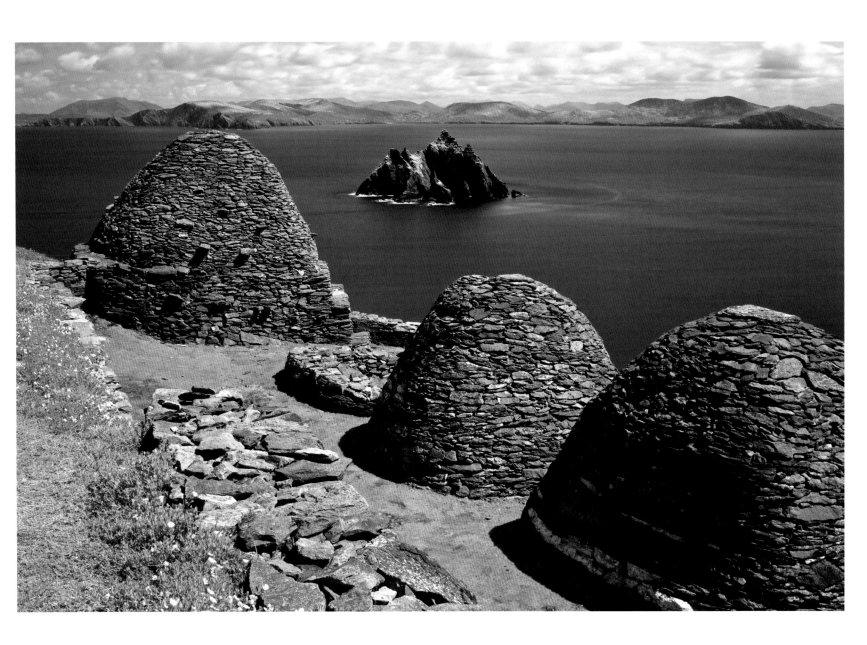

**Above**: *Monastery on Great Skellig with Little Skellig in the background, County Kerry.*

**Below**: Templenoe Pier, Kenmare River, County Kerry

**Opposite**: Between sea and sky, Slea Head and Blasket Islands, County Kerry

**Opposite bottom**: Flat topshell

The Blaskets are an island group off Slea Head on the Dingle Peninsula. In the 1920s and 1930s several books emerged from the community of the Great Blasket, written in the Irish language and describing everyday life on the island.

Peig Sayers, Muiris Ó Súilleabháin and Tomás Ó Criomhtháin are probably the best known and their books *Peig*, *Twenty Years A-Growing* and *The Islandman* have been translated into several languages and are deemed classics in literature.

There never was a big community on the Great Blasket. At its height in 1916 the population reached no more than 176 people and after that it declined steadily mainly due to emigration. In 1953 the last remaining twenty-two inhabitants left the Great Blasket for good.

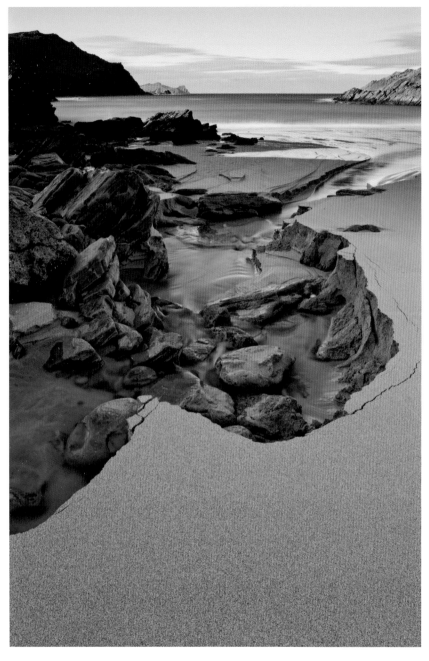

*Left*: *Clogher Strand, Dingle Peninsula, County Kerry*
*Opposite*: *The Dingle Seal and Wildlife Sanctuary, County Kerry*

The Irish Seal Sanctuary is dedicated to the rescue and rehabilitation of all marine wildlife but is, as the name suggests, particularly concerned with abandoned, injured, distressed or malnourished seals.

The ISS was founded in 1986 by Brendan Price, who was also a founding member of the *Irish Whale and Dolphin Group*. For 20 years the ISS was run out of Brendan's back garden in Balbriggan, Co. Dublin. After Fingal County Council withdrew the funding for a planned marine conservation facility the ISS had to start looking for a new home.

In 2006 the sanctuary was eventually offered a three-acre site close to the beach at the Gorey-Courtown Forest Park in County Wexford. The plan was not only to extend the facilities but also built a visitor center, which would create vital funding for the ISS.

In 2011 however staff of the sanctuary

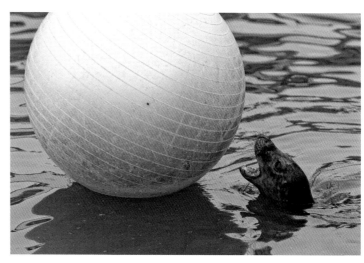

found themselves locked out of the facility after an escalating dispute between the owners of the site and the ISS. At the time of writing the ISS is still homeless and most of the rescued seals are treated at the *Dingle Wildlife and Seal Sanctuary*. At times, it can seem like groups like the ISS are fighting a losing battle against cruelty and ignorance: the heads of two slaughtered seals were nailed at the entrance of the *Dingle Seal and Wildlife Sanctuary* in summer 2012, where I had photographed the work of the I*rish*

*Seal Sanctuary* only weeks earlier. To date the ISS and its volunteers have rescued and treated more than eight hundred seals and are dealing with more than two thousand distress calls every year. In addition the ISS has made a real difference through an education program for schools and regular eco walks and talks; it is to be hoped that work of this kind will continue to change some people's attitudes towards the other creatures who share our world.

**Below**: Rossbehy Strand, Iveragh Peninsula, County Kerry

**Opposite**: Abandoned houses and Blasket Islands, Dingle Peninsula, County Kerry

**Below** : *Dingle Peninsula from Fenit, County Kerry*

***Above***: *Derrymore Strand, Dingle Peninsula, County Kerry*

**Above**: *Cliffs and fog, Loop Head, County Clare*

# THE WEST

The west, incorporating the counties Clare and Galway, is probably the most diverse part of Ireland's coast. The very south west of County Clare is formed by the Loop Head Peninsula, which borders at the estuary of Ireland's longest river, the Shannon. An incredible variety of habitats and landforms can be found here, mudflats, salt marshes, rocky and sandy shores and cliffs with sea stacks, rock arches and sea caves.

The relatively dcep water and shelter from the Atlantic Ocean has made the Shannon Estuary an important centre for industry, imports and exports for Ireland. The industry includes two major power-generation plants at Moneypoint, County Clare and Tarbert, County Kerry and deep-water ports at Foynes and Limerick, which can accommodate vessels up to 20,0000 dwt (dead-weight tonnage).

In addition both sides of the estuary are dotted with countless fishing and leisure ports. Boat-based Dolphin Watching has become a major tourist attraction and during spring and summer regular tours leave from Kilrush and Carrigaholt on the Clare side of the estuary.

Once the Loop Head peninsula joins the mainland at the seaside resort of Kilkee, Clare's coast becomes a mix of rocky shores, cliffs and some of Ireland's finest surfing beaches like Lahinch and Spanish Point. North west of Lahinch, on a plateau that provides fine views over Clare's coast and countryside, lies one of the country's major tourist attractions: The Cliffs of Moher, eight kilometres of sheer rock dropping into the Atlantic Ocean.

From here on the coastal scenery changes dramatically. The Burren is a limestone karst landscape renowed for its mingling of mediterranean, arctic and alpine flora and strange appearance. A mainly rocky shoreline is overlooked by grey, terrace shaped hills dotted with erratic bouders. There is, however, a break in the wild rocky shoreline at Fanore, where there is a broad sandy beach and adjoining dune system. Off the Burren coast the three Aran Islands lie like sleeping giants in the Atlantic Ocean: Inishmore, Inishsheer and Inishman are part of County Galway, but geologically they are an outpost of the limestone moonscape of the Burren.

Just north of Fanore the coastline makes a sharp eastern turn and opens up into Galway Bay. The eastern part of the bay that eventually leads to Galway City is a taste of things to come: small bays, peninsulas and islands form a calmer, more serene seascape.

Just outside the limits of Galway City lie the borders of one of Ireland's most famous landscapes: Connemara, named after 'Conmhaicne Mara', 'the descendants of the sea', is an incredible rugged landscape. A bird's-eye view looks like a giant has ripped out bits and pieces from the landscape, leaving behind torn and jagged fringes. Connemara's coastline twists and turns, forming countless small bays and tiny inlets, peninsulas and islands, which make exploring this unique place the challenge of a lifetime.

*Opposite*: Shannon Estuary at Killimer, County Clare **Above**: Foynes Harbour,
County Limerick **Below** : Kilbaha Harbour, County Clare

**Above**: *The Shannon Bottlenose Dolphins*

**Opposite**: *Common Seals, Kilbaha Bay, County Clare*

The Shannon Estuary is an incredible place for wildlife. Despite the fact that it is a major shipping lane with two major industrial ports at Foynes and Limerick and several smaller harbours along the way, nature is thriving here. The estuary is a feeding ground for thousands of seabirds; some nest on the cliffs of the Loop Head Peninsula, while some, like the gannet, come from as far away as the Skelligs to feed. Both common and grey seals live and breed in the area and the white coats of newborn grey seals are a regular sight in the storm caves around Loop Head.

The biggest attraction, however, is Ireland's only resident population of bottlenose dolphins. More than a hundred animals, locally known as the 'Shannon Dolphins', live in the area, taking advantage of the strong tidal currents that bring a constant food supply. Legends of sea monsters dating back many centuries might suggest that the dolphins' presence is no recent thing.

*Opposite*: Thrift, Loop Head, County Clare

*Above*: Oyster Beds, College Strand, Loop Head Peninsula, County Clare

*Below*: Woody nightshade

71

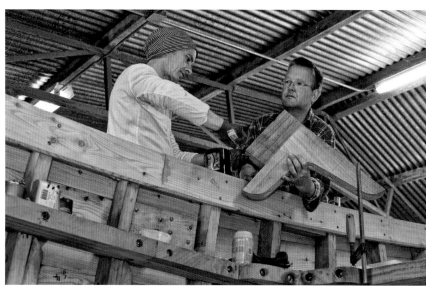

**Above**: *Building the Sally O'Keeffe, Querrin, County Clare*
**Opposite**: *Sally O'Keeffe maiden journey, Shannon estuary, County Clare*

The tradition of boat building is still very strong in Ireland and traditional boats like the currach or the Galway hooker are a regular sight around Ireland's coast. Some boats, however, have almost disappeared into the mists of time. The wooden sailing boat of the Shannon Estuary, the Shannon Hooker, is one of them. They were once regular transport for people, livestock, turf, fish and other cargo up and down the estuary.

In 2010 the *Seol Sionna* project, whose name means 'Shannon Sail', was born to bring the traditional sailing boats back to the Shannon. In the small village of Querrin, which once had a fleet of twenty-five of these boats, the Sally O'Keeffe was built over a period of almost two years. Named after the lady who owned one of the last turf boats in the area in the 1800s, the Shannon hooker made a proud return to the waters of the Shannon on 19 May 2012.

*Below* : *Kilbaha Bay, County Clare*

**Above**: *Winter Storm, Loop Head, County Clare*

***Above****: Carrigaholt Castle, Shannon Estuary, County Clare*

*Below : Ross, Loop Head Peninsula, County Clare*

*Below* : Kilkee Strand and West End, County Clare

*Opposite top*: The Strand Races, Kilkee, County Clare

*Opposite bottom*: Snakelocks Anemone

Around 150 years ago Kilkee was nothing more than a small fishing village, but when the wealthy aristocrats and merchants from the nearby city of Limerick started building summer residencies at the West End of the village, Kilkee started to attract visitors. During the eighteenth century Kilkee became one of the most famous seaside resorts in Ireland and still attracts thousands of visitors during the summer months.

Surrounded by sheer cliffs Kilkee's main attraction is the horseshoe-shaped beach, where horse races – the 'Strand Races' – are held every autumn. The beach is protected from the full force of the Atlantic by the Dugerrna Reef that stretches across the mouth of the bay. The reef is also home to the 'Pollock Holes', swimming-pool-sized rock pools that are very popular places to swim at low tide.

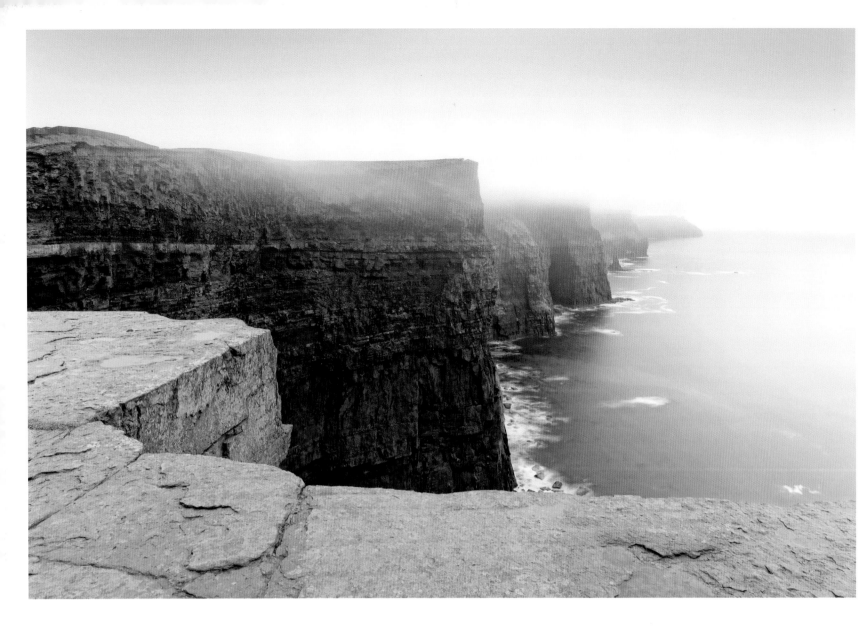

Waves that left America roll up the base

Of these huge tapestries of stone,

Voices from the coffin ships mutter

And thunder at their base

Beating the drums of under sea jungles.

*Mike Harding, from 'The Cliffs of Moher'*

**Above**: *Cliffs of Moher, County Clare*
**Opposite**: *Black Head Lighthouse and Galway Bay, The Burren, County Clare*

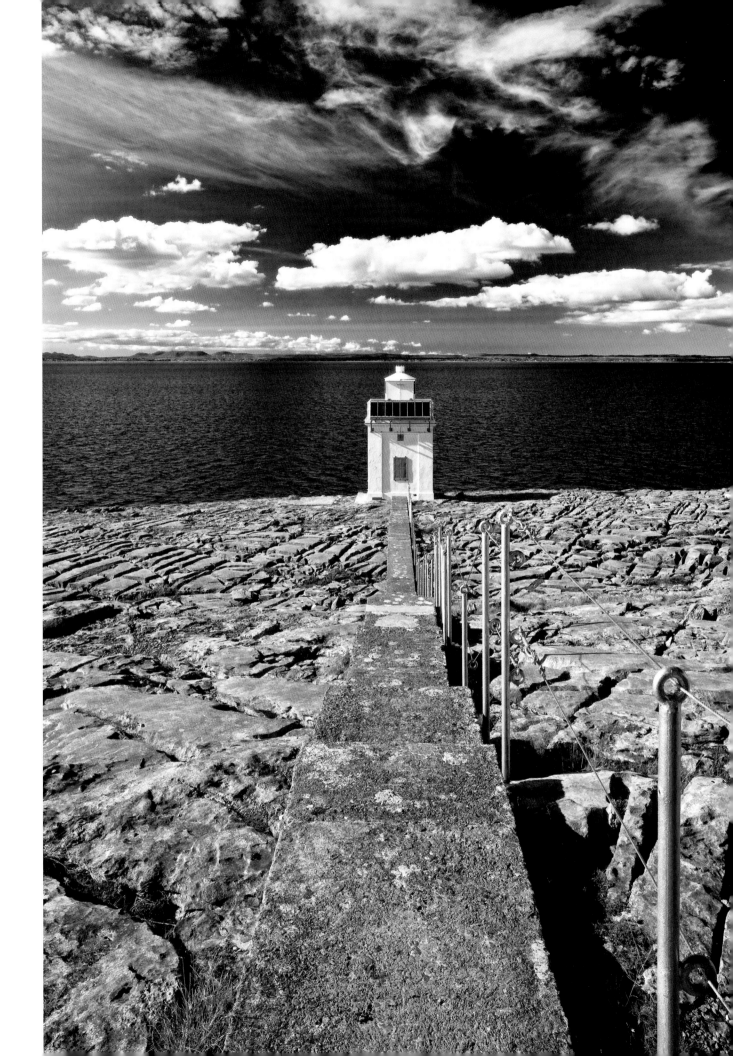

**Below** : Ballyryan, The Burren, County Clare

***Above**: Aughinish and New Quay, The Burren, County Clare*

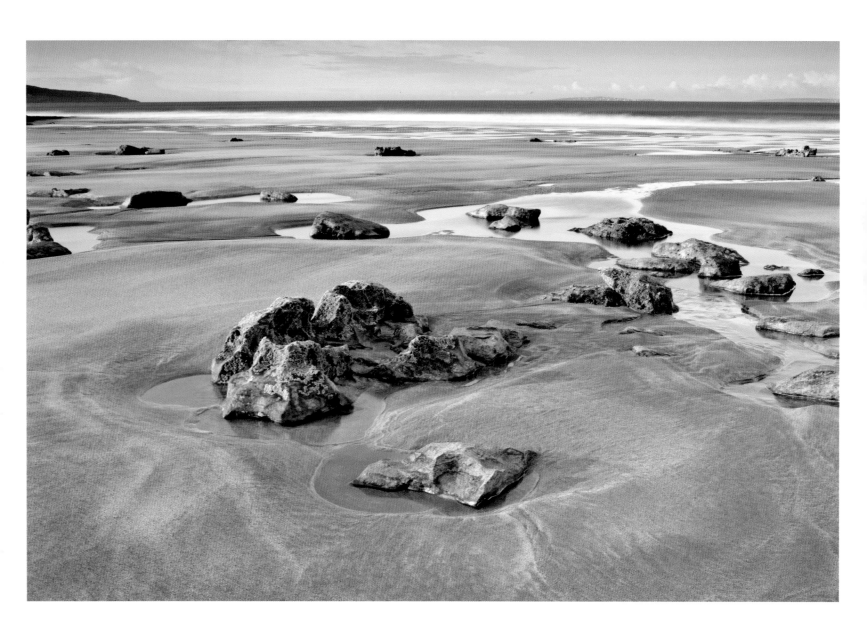

**Above**: *Fanore Strand, The Burren, County Clare*

*Below* : *Aran Islands seen from Black Head, The Burren, County Clare*

*Above*: Galway Hookers, Kinvara, County Galway
*Opposite*: Dunguaire Castle, Kinvara, County Galway

The Cruinniu na mBád is one of many traditional boat festivals that are held in Ireland every year. The star of Cruinniu na mBád, 'the gathering of the boats', is the Galway hooker and to see a whole fleet of them, with their distinctive red sails, is an inspiring sight.

The Galway Hookers are subdivided into four types. The largest vessel, the Bád Mór, or 'large boat', is up to thirteen metres in length. The second largest, the Leath Bhád, or 'half-boat', reaches around ten metres. The other two boats are the small Gleoiteog and the diminutive Púcán. All of them were working boats used to carry all kinds of cargo, but mainly turf and fish, around the Burren and Connemara coast. The bigger boats were able to hold loads of up to fifteen tonnes.

As part of the Cruinniú na mBád festival, a load of turf is delivered to Kinvara by hooker to honour the traditional use of the boat.

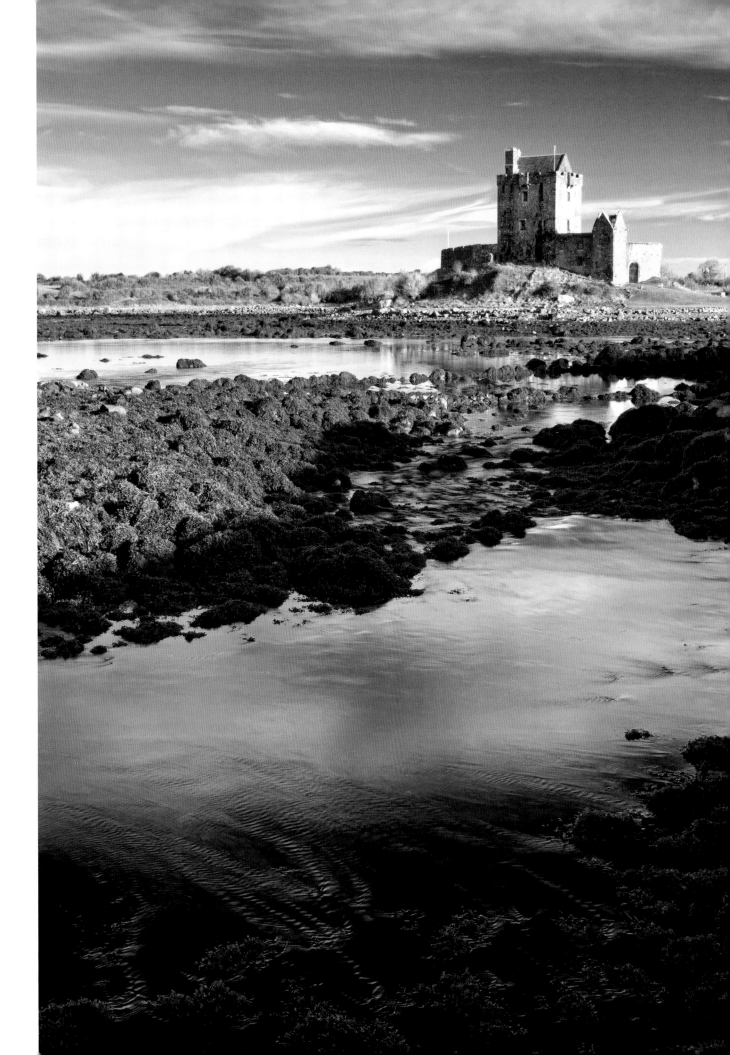

**Below** : Marina, Galway Docks, County Galway

***Above***: *Galway Bay, Connemara, County Galway*

The Claddagh, from the Irish 'cladach' meaning 'stony beach', was once a fishing village at the edges of Galway City. Despite its proximity to the city the Claddagh was a closed community with its own customs, traditions, laws and even its own king.

For centuries the Claddagh fishermen dominated the fishing industry around Galway Bay. The Claddagh community was also one of few that managed to continue their traditional way of life and Irish language and maintain the distinctive look of their village – thatched cottages and cobbled streets – long into the English suppression.

Change however begun in the early 1900s when modern trawlers started to fish in Galway bay. Around the same time living conditions in the village were declared unsafe and cottage after cottage was being knocked down. Over the following decades the face of the Claddagh changed distinctively and today it is firmly integrated into the greater Galway City area. What remain, however, are stories and legends and the famous Claddagh Ring, a distinctive piece of jewellery shaped like two hands joining together to hold a heart topped with a crown; it has been around since the 1700s, but its origins have been lost in time.

*Opposite top*: The Claddagh, Galway, County Galway
*Below*: Spiddal, Connemara, County Galway

**Above**: Camus Bay, Connemara, County Galway

**Below** : *Culfin Estuary and Mweelrea Mountains, Connemara, County Galway*

*Below* : Coral Strand, Mannin Bay, Connemara, County Galway

**Opposite**: **Bottom left** : Cleggan shore, Connemara, County Galway. **Top left** : Coral strand, Connemara, County Galway. **Top right** : Sand patterns, Connemara, County Galway. **Bottom right** : Sand and rock, Inishmore, County Galway

*Above*: Moyrus, Carna, Connemara, County Galway

*Opposite top*: Netted Dog Whelk

*Opposite bottom*: Gurteen Bay, Roundstone, Connemara, County Galway

Connemara, and especially its coast, was the first Irish landscape I explored extensively with my camera. During my first year as an Irish resident I was working as a tour guide in Connemara which gave me the chance to get up close and personal with this most unique place. Long summer evenings at Ballyconneely, waiting for the tide to retreat, walking over the vast stretch of sand that connects Omey island with the mainland at low tide and exploring the seaweed covered foreshores around Carna are just a few of many fond memories.

I have returned countless times since then, but so far Connemara hasn't lost its magic. Once this timeless landscape with its sinuous and jagged shores has cast its spell, you will long to return.

*Opposite*: Ballyconneely, Connemara, County Galway
*Above*: Gora Mór, Connemara, County Galway

**Below**: Derryinver Bay, Connemara, County Galway

**Opposite top**: Old pier, Killary, Connemara

**Opposite bottom**: Painted topshell

Killary Harbour came to fame as Ireland's only fjord. It winds its way sixteen kilometres from the open Atlantic to the village of Lenaun.

According to definition a fjord is a long, narrow, deep inlet of the sea between high cliffs, typically formed by submergence of a glaciated valley – Killary Harbour is certainly long and narrow, and reaches a depth of forty-five metres. Over the years there has been discussion about what constitutes a fjord – mainly because the 'fjord' in Scandinavia, where the word originated, differs somewhat from what is understood to be a fjord in the rest of Europe – but at the moment Killary is considered to be one of three fjords in Ireland, the other two being Carlingford Lough in County Louth and Lough Swilly in County Donegal.

But I wouldn't be surprised if this would change again. In the end it doesn't really matter, Killary is one of the most enchanting parts of Connemara's coast, fjord or no fjord.

**Above**: *White Strand, Tully, Connemara, County Galway*

**Below** : Sellerna Bay, Connemara, County Galway

**Above**: *Burning Sky, Streedagh Strand, County Sligo*

# THE NORTH WEST

The counties Mayo, Sligo, Leitrim and Donegal form the northwestern coast of Ireland. This is probably the wildest and most dramatic part of the coast, battered by gales and storms more often than the rest of the country; in December 2011 a 20.4 metre-high wave was recorded off the Donegal coast, at the time the highest ever recorded.

For me, the northwest begins just north of Killary Harbour and the Mweelrea Mountains. A string of seemingly endless sandy beaches runs up to Carrickyvegraly Point where the coastline makes a sharp turn east and opens up into Clew Bay. According to legend the wide bay is dotted with 365 islands, one for each day of the year. These islands are sunken drumlins, small hills that were formed by retreating glaciers, and in

reality there are only around 117 of them. The northern entry to the bay is guarded by the Curaun peninsula and Ireland's biggest and probably most famous island: Achill. Overlooking Clew Bay is Croagh Patrick, locally known as 'the Reek', Ireland's holy mountain. According to legend, St Patrick fasted there for forty days in the fifth century. Today every last Sunday of July several thousand pilgrims climb the Reek, rain or shine.

North of Achill the coast is rugged, wandering inland to form bays or to follow river estuaries. At Benwee Head, one of the most breathtaking headlands the coast turns east once again. Beyond that lies mile after mile of head-spinning cliffs that only run out at Killala Bay. This funnel-shaped bay became famous as landing place for the

**Above**: Clew Bay and Croagh Patrick, County Mayo

French, who came to help the Irish with their fight for independence from British rule during the 1798 rebellion.

Further east lies Sligo Bay, overlooked by the enigmatic shapes of Sligo's mountains and resting place of W. B. Yeats one of Ireland's most famous poets. Here the coast runs northward again, with rocky shores and some of Ireland's best-known surf-ing beaches like Bundoran, until it reaches Donegal Bay.

The Donegal coastline is home to some of the most remote and rugged places in Ireland. The hump of the Slieve League Peninsula with its spellbinding cliffs is followed by river estuaries, bays, inlets and clusters of islands, which are the main features of Donegal's west coast. This area is Ireland's biggest *Gaeltacht*

(Irish-speaking) area.

North Donegal is dominated by sea loughs that penetrate far inland: Mulroy Bay, Lough Swilly and Lough Foyle. In-between are windswept headlands like Melmore Head, Fanad Head and – laying claim to the title of mainland Ireland's most northerly point – Malin Head. Geographically, however, this title belongs to Banba's Crown north-east of Malin Head. Ireland's true north is Inishtrahull Island and even further north are the Torr Rocks at 55° 27' 03" North.

**Below** : Clare Island from Bunowen Strand, County Mayo

'*An Gorta Mór*' – 'the great hunger' – better known as the Great Famine is an event that changed and defined Ireland; in the years between 1845 and 1852 it's estimated that a million people starved to death and another million or more emigrated, reducing the Irish population by around a quarter.

Those who were able to leave crossed the Atlantic Ocean to seek a better life in the USA or Canada on what became known as Famine Ships or Coffin Ships. Conditions on these ships were anything but good:

'*Hundreds of poor people, men, women and children of all ages huddled together without light, without air, wallowing in filth and breathing a fetid atmosphere, sick in body, dispirited in heart; the fevered patients lying beside the sound, by their agonised ravings disturbing those around …*'

(Stephen de Vere, who sailed to America in steerage in 1847).

Almost half of the people heading for the New World lost their life on the journey.

**Opposite**: *Famine Memorial, Murrisk, County Mayo*
**Above**: *Keem Strand, Achill Island, County Mayo*

**Below** : Pollagh Harbour, Achill Island, County Mayo

**Opposite top**: Barnynagappul Strand, Achill Island, County Mayo

**Opposite bottom**: Sea Rocket

Achill is Ireland's largest off-shore island and has been and still is a favorite with artists, including photographers, for centuries. The British novelist Graham Greene wrote parts of his novel *The Heart of the Matter* and *The Fallen Idol* in the village of Dooagh. The German author and Nobel Prize winner Heinrich Böll was a regular visitor to Achill in the 1950s and 1960s and he documented his visits in what became one of his best loved books *Irisches Tagebuch / Irish Journal*. Böll's cottage is now a retreat for artists and writers. One of America's foremost painters, Paul Henri, also owned a house on Achill where he painted mainly portraits of local people and Ulster-born painter Paul Henry lived and worked on Achill for a decade where, it is said, he first found his inspiration for his famous West of Ireland landscape paintings.

The Mullet Peninsula, also known as The Mullet, is a long and narrow promontory that is connected to the mainland only by a small isthmus at its northern end. The Mullet's southern part is a flat and windswept place with wide sandy beaches and rocky shores. In the North the landscape rises up to form the exposed cliffs of Erris Head that allow dramatic views over the North Mayo landscape. On my visits the weather came with cloud, wind and showers, the kind of weather that seems tailor-made for this beautiful and sad landscape.

This is how the Mullet looks today and judging by the description the Irish naturalist Robert Lloyd Praeger gave in the early 1900s nothing much has changed since then:

'Belmullet lies on an absurdly narrow isthmus which separates Broad Haven on the North from the much larger and deeper bay of Blacksod on the South, and almost makes an island of the Mullet. Blacksod Bay has low and rather desolate shores on either side, but Broad Haven, though more sterile, is more attractive, as the Atlantic waves, beating into it, have carved a boulder coastline, which outside the bay becomes very grand … The Mullet, that remote peninsula, half bog, half sand, full of bays and queer lakes and outlying islets; tree-less, sodden, storm swept, and everywhere pounded by the besieging sea, beautiful on a fine day, with wondrous colour over land and ocean, desolate beyond words when the Atlantic rain drives across the shelterless surface.'

(from *The Way That I Went* by Robert Lloyd Praeger 1865–1953)

**Opposite top**: Elly Bay, Mullet Peninsula, County Mayo
**Opposite bottom**: Strawberry Anemone
**Below**: Blacksod Bay, Mullet Peninsula, County Mayo

*Opposite*: Gateway, Erris Head, County Mayo
**Above**: Moyne Abbey, Killala Bay, County Mayo

Moyne Abbey is one of Ireland's best-preserved monasteries and the fact that the monastic grounds are overlooking Killala Bay gave me a welcome excuse to include this amazing place in this book.

The abbey was founded by permission of Pope Nicholas for the Observantine Franciscans around 1460 and consists of several buildings including a sacristy, a chapter house, kitchen and refectory and an almost intact tower.

In its heyday Moyne Abbey was home to around fifty monks. After several raids in the late 1500s, during which parts of the friary were burned down, the community dispersed. Over the succeeding centuries only a handful of monks kept the friary alive and it is thought that the last friar of Moyne, Fr Thomas Burke, died in 1800.

**Below** : *Soft morning, Killala Bay, County Mayo*

***Above****: Stormy Weather, Downpatrick Head, County Mayo*

**Above**: *Benwee Head, County Mayo*

*Below* : *Aughris Head, County Sligo*

**Bottom Left**: *Spiny Starfish*. **Top Left**: *Seven Armed Starfish*.
**Top Right**: *Bloody Henry*. **Bottom Right**: *Common Starfish*

**Left**: *Common Sea Urchin* **Right**: *Beadlet Anemone*

Rock pools, or tidal pools, are a colourful microcosmos of marine life and can be found on many rocky shores all around the Irish coast with some of the finest examples along the shores of the west and northwest. Twice a day the retreating tide leaves behind not only exposed rock surfaces, but also water-filled crevices, hollows and pools.

These sanctuaries are home to mussels, crabs, starfish, urchins, shrimps, fish and countless other fauna and flora. These plants and animals are among the hardiest on the planet. They have to endure extreme fluctuations in water temperature, salinity and oxygen levels. Huge waves, strong currents and the exposure to predators and 'rock-pooling' homo sapiens, including eager photographers, are just a few of the hazards they have to cope with on a daily basis.

*Below* : Mullaghmore Harbour, County Sligo

*Opposite top*: Enniscrone Cliff Baths and Strand, County Sligo

*Opposite bottom*: Kidney Vetch

Enniscrone is one of Ireland's major seaside resorts built around a wide sandy beach with adjoining dunes and indispensable golf course. Resorts like Enniscrone developed during the Victorian era to cater for the holiday needs of the upper class and the rich. The old cliff bath, built in 1850 in typical Victorian style, is an elegant reminder of this era.

Today towns like Bray, Tramore, Kilkee or Ballycastle, to name but a few others, attract visitors from abroad and Irish tourists alike and offer a multitude of amenities. Unfortunately all of these towns suffer one common fate: The big hustle and bustle of the summer months disappears rather suddenly in early autumn and most resorts become ghost towns for the winter months.

**Above**: *Trawgar, Streedagh, County Sligo*

*Below* : Illaunee Beg, Mullaghmore, County Sligo

**Above**: Incoming tide, Bundoran, County Donegal

The origins of surfing can be found somewhere in the Pacific Ocean some three thousand years ago. Many archeologists believe that ancient Peru is the cradle of surfing; pottery found there shows people riding on waves on what very much resemble surfboards. These devices that are thought to have been halfway between a boat and a surfboard, called *Caballito de Totora*, were most likely made out of buoyant reeds.

The first Europeans to witness surfing were the crew of the HMS *Endeavour* under captain James Cook in 1769 when they landed on Polynesia. For many Polynesian cultures the art of surfing was much more than just a recreational sport – it was a part of their heritage and spiritual beliefs. Priests were integral part of the ritual, blessing new boards and praying to the gods for good surf.

James Cook and his men were followed soon after by western missionaries who suppressed surfing and other local traditions for many decades. The art of surfing almost became forgotten.

In the early twentieth century, how-

***Above****: Bundoran Surfers, County Donegal*

ever, surfing was rediscovered by Westerners almost simultaneously in America and Australia. Subsequently it also saw a revival in its native Hawaii. The rest is, as they say, history.

The very first Irish surfer was probably Joe Roddy, son of a lighthouse keeper on Ireland's east coast, who rode the waves off Dundalk on a self-made board sometime around 1949.

Kevin Cavey and Ian Hill however were the ones who firmly established an Irish surf scene in the 1960s and today Ireland is one of the surf capitals of the world. It is said that Irish beaches like Inch Strand, Lahinch, Keel or Bundoran, have the best surf outside Hawaii. In 2011 the European Championships came to Ireland for the first time and were held in Bundoran.

**Below** : Murvagh Forest, County Donegal

**Left**: *Thrift & Lichen, County Donegal.* **Right**: *Dune Flora, County Donegal*

*Below* : *Killybegs Harbour, County Donegal*

*Opposite top*: *Mute Swans, Clew Bay, County Mayo.*
*Opposite bottom*: *Black Backed and Herring Gulls, feeding frenzy, County Donegal*

**Below**: *Loughros More Bay, County Donegal*
**Opposite top**: *Maghera Caves, County Donegal*
**Opposite bottom**: *Sheep's Bit*

The caves at Maghera Beach have been formed by the relentless power of the tides and are surrounded by many tales and mysteries. One time it is said a man and his dog entered the caves. Sometime later the dog emerged several miles away at Glen-colmcille, the man however has never been seen again. Another story tells us about five hundred or so Irish rebels and their families hiding in the caves. To mark the birth of a child a candle was placed in one of the cave entrances. This light was seen across the bay and alarmed the occupying English forces. It is said that all but one man were slaughtered that night.

**Below** : *Eddie's Boat, Bunbeg, County Donegal*

In the early 1970s the *Bád Eddie*, 'Eddie's Boat', ran aground at the sheltered bay of Magherclogher where it has become one of Ireland's most photographed shipwrecks and has become a Bunbeg landmark.

***Above****: Sunset, Fanad, County Donegal*

Slieve League reaches a height of six hundred metres and is among the highest sea cliffs in Europe. Getting there is an adventure in itself. A few kilometers west of Killybegs the traveler enters a net of small country roads that wind southwards along Teelin Bay and then turn west into and over the mountains. The last stretch of road twists and turns in a steep up and down fashion along a narrow ridge. The road is hardly wide enough for one car and there is nowhere to pull in. I expected to take a tumble into the abyss beside the road any moment and prayed that there might be no oncoming traffic.

Slieve League itself almost defies description. It is literally land's end. There is mountain and sea and nothing more. Its remoteness, majesty and beauty make Slieve League an extraordinary place. If there only wasn't the way back along that road.

**Opposite top**: *Common Limpet*

**Opposite bottom**: *Slieve League, County Donegal*

**Above**: *Crohy Head, County Donegal*

***Above****: Jeffrey's Lough, Ards Forest, County Donegal*
***Opposite****: Fanad Head Lighthouse, County Donegal*

In 1812 the frigate *Saldana* was wrecked at the treacherous rocks of Fanad Head, which was known as Fannett Point back then, leaving a parrot as the only survivor. This tragedy resulted in the decision to built a lighthouse and Fanad Lighthouse was subsequently lit for the first time on 17 March 1817. Dramatically situated on a rocky outcrop, Fanad Lighthouse watches over both the Fanad headland and the entrance to Lough Swilly.

**Below** : *Urris Hills and dunes, Inishowen Peninsula, County Donegal*

**Above**: *Fog on Lough Swilly, Inishowen Peninsula, County Donegal*

**Above**: *Drumlins at Strangford lough, County Down*
**Page 144**: *Giant's Causeway, County Antrim*
**Page 145**: *Dunluce Castle, County Antrim*

# THE NORTH EAST

The north eastern corner of Ireland boasts two very different, but equally breathtaking landscapes – the jaw-dropping drama of the Antrim coast and the softer, more rounded landscape of the Strangford Lough area.

The Antrim coast looks like something from the epic novels of J.R.R. Tolkien and C.S. Lewis, which is perhaps unsurprising when one realises that Lewis was born in Belfast and spent his childhood summers on the north east coast. Rugged cliffs, rock arches and sea stacks intertwine with wide, sandy beaches and boulder-strewn bays. The whole area is sprinkled with historic castles and monasteries. It is not surprising that the Causeway Coastal Route, which runs from Portrush to Carrickfergus, can regularly be found among the world's top scenic drives.

The mysterious Dunluce Castle and the wide sandy beach of Whitepark Bay can all be found along this route.

As can the Giant's Causeway, probably the most famous part of the Antrim coast. This natural causeway is made of an estimated 40,000 hexagonal basalt columns stretching out into the ocean and was formed during a long period of volcanic activity some sixty million years ago. That is if you believe the scientists.

Legend tells us a more colourful theory and attributes the causeway to the giant Finn McCool. Finn had a mortal enemy in Benandonnar, a giant living on the Scottish island of Staffa. Both giants decided to build a road across the ocean, Finn starting in Antrim, Benandonnar starting on Staffa.

The two giants eventually met in the

middle, but the resulting fight unfortunately destroyed most of their handiwork.
All that remains today is the Giant's Causeway in Antrim and a smaller causeway at Fingal's Cave on Staffa.

However, the best sights as far as I am concerned, are slightly off the main track. Fair
Head seen from Murlough Bay is probably
my favourite view in Ireland and manages to
amaze me every time I return

This also goes for Rathlin Island, which lies
a short boat trip off the Antrim coast. Like
all of Antrim this island is full of history and
legends. Robert the Bruce supposedly had

his life changing encounter with a spider in a
cave on Rathlin. Legend tells us that Robert
the Bruce was on the run, his army scattered
after having lost six battles against the English invaders. Robert eventually fled to Rathlin where he hid in a cave and contemplated
his fate. One rainy day he was watching a
spider weave her web. He watched her working slowly and with care, trying to throw her
thread from one end of the cave to the other.
Six times she tried, six times she failed. 'Poor
creature,' said Robert the Bruce, 'you too
know how it feels to fail six times in a row.'
The spider, however, didn't give up and her

seventh attempt was successful. It is said that the little spider's determination inspired him not to give up. He gathered his forces again and eventually Scotland became independent and Robert the Bruce king of Scotland.

Strangford Lough to the south of Antrim couldn't be visually more different. This sea lough, formed by retreating glaciers some ten thousand years ago, is a soft and understated affair. The landscape of Strangford is dominated by drumlins – distinctive round hills made of glacial deposits – muddy shores and scattered islands.

The lough stretches from the wide, calm mudflats of the north for thirty-two kilometres to the so called 'Narrows' in the south. Here the Irish Sea enters and leaves Strangford Lough with powerful tidal currents, carrying about 350 million cubic metres of water with every tide. Early Viking invaders called the place 'Strangfjörthr', 'the strong fjord'.

Strangford Lough is one of the most peaceful and calming places I know and spending a summer afternoon at Reagh Island, watching the tide come and go, is one of my most treasured memories.

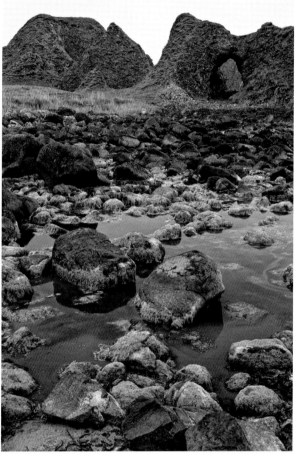

***Opposite***: *Elephant Rock, Ballintoy, County Antrim*

***Above left***: *Grey Heron and Basalt Rocks, Ballintoy, County Antrim*

***Above right***: *Red tide, Ballintoy, County Antrim.*

The Arcadia Café has a long and colourful history to look back on. Built on a rocky outcrop in the 1920s by a local businessman, R. E. Chalmers, it soon became a thriving seaside café. In 1953 a ballroom was added that saw many of the at the time very popular showbands and in the seventies it even attracted rock acts like The Stranglers and The Undertones. The ballroom is gone now, but the café is still open and bustling.

*Opposite*: Arcadia Café, Portrush, County Antrim

*Below* : Beach fun, Portrush, County Antrim

One of the many brochures I acquired during my travels is entitled Portrush Rocks and this title sums it up nicely for the whole of the Antrim coast.

Even to the visitor who couldn't care less about geology and rocks it becomes apparent that something extraordinary must have happened here. Dark black stones lie side by side with pure white ones and in some places dark red and brown rocks join the party.

The oldest rocks in the area are clays and schists which were formed around 190 million years ago. During the Cretaceous Age, which ended around 65 million years ago, sandstones and limestones, including chalk were laid down on top of the older rocks. The soft chalk deposits have disappeared from most of Ireland, but have survived in Antrim due to being covered and protected by lava. Several major lava flows between 62 and 56 million years ago covered Antrim with a thick layer of basalt. This basalt was partly worn away by the glaciers of the ice age while continuous volcanic eruptions intruded into the older rocks forming what is known as volcanic plugs.

Faulting, shifts in the relative level of the land caused by earthquakes, did the rest and brought older rocks to the same level as new rock formations. The result is a colourful and utterly fascinating rock garden.

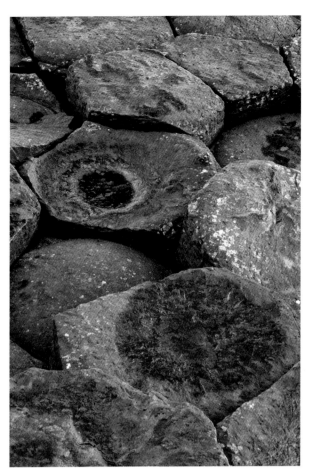

*Opposite*: Whitepark Bay and Portbradden, County Antrim **Bottom left**: Chalk, Larry Bane Bay, County Antrim **Top left**: Sandstone, Murlough Bay, County Antrim. **Top right**: Basalt Columns, Giant's Causeway, County Antrim. **Bottom right**: Sandstone, Colliery Bay, County Antrim

***Above****: Larry Bane Bay, County Antrim*

***Opposite****: Tree and Fair Head, Murlough Bay, County Antrim*

**Below** : Pans Rock, Ballycastle, County Antrim

***Above****: Ballycastle Beach with Rathlin Island, County Antrim*

Kinbane Castle is situated on a limestone headland protruding out into Rathlin Sound. Overlooking the headland and small bay are steep basalt cliffs. This is a magical and haunting location, especially when darkness approaches the shadows of the past seem to come alive.

Under the headland lies a sea cave which is known as *Lag na Sassenach*, 'the hollow of the English'; the name is believed to come from an incident in the 1500s, when a garrison of English soldiers was laying siege to the castle. The occupants of the castle lit a fire on the headland and soon help came from all directions. The English soldiers became trapped between sea and cliffs and legend has it every single one of them was slaughtered.

*Opposite top*: Kinbane Castle, County Antrim
*Opposite bottom*: Sea campion
*Below*: Ballintoy Harbour, County Antrim

*Opposite*: The lazy bunch; grey seals on Rathlin Island, County Antrim

*Below* : East lighthouse, Rathlin Island, County Antrim

**Above**: *Old Pier, Red Bay, County Antrim*

**Opposite bottom**: *Beadlet Anemone*

**Opposite top**: *Cushendall and Tievebulliagh, Red Bay, County Antrim*

Although this is a book about the coast this chapter wouldn't be complete without mentioning the Glens of Antrim, as they are such an integral and well-known part of the region.

Each of the nine Glens of Antrim has its own character, mirrored in names like Glencloy, *the glen of the hedges*, Glenariff, *the fertile glen* or Glendun, *the glen of the brown river*.

*Opposite top*: Yachts at Red Bay, County Antrim. ***Opposite bottom***: Belfast Docks, County Antrim ***Above***: Nendrum Monastery, County Down

On Mahee Island, which can be reached via long and twisting roads and causeways, lies Nendrum Monastery. Although not much is left beside foundation walls this is an inspiring place and the reason why the early Christian monks choose this location soon becomes clear; the heart of the monastery, church and round tower, stand on top of a drumlin with breathtaking views in all directions. Yet it is a secluded location which I assume could be reached only by boat or a long walk across the mud at low tide back then. The origins of Nendrum are somewhat unclear but it is believed that St Machaoi founded the monastery in the fifth century and later a Benedictine cell was established which lasted from the twelfth to the fifteenth century.

**Below** : *Reagh Island, Strangford Lough, County Down*

**Above**: *Donaghadee Harbour, Ards Peninsula, County Down*

**Above**: Vico Baths, County Dublin

# THE EAST

Looking at a map of Ireland the eastern seaboard might appear almost boring, running in a more or less straight line from County Louth in the north to County Wicklow in the south. But although the rough drama of the west coast is missing here the shores of the Irish Sea hold other, more subtle, qualities.

Louth, also known as 'the Wee County', is probably best known for the gentle beauty of the Cooley Peninsula and Carlingford Lough with its views over to County Down where, to use the words of Percy French, 'the Mountains of Mourne sweep down to the sea'.

For me, however, the real beauty of the Louth coast lies further south. Wide sandy beaches and mudflats are only intercepted by a few rocky headlands and river estuar-

ies. One of my favorite places on this stretch of coast is the Boyne estuary. It offers an extensive dune system and adjoining sandy beach with a rich wildlife and, as a special treat, the wreck of MV *Irish Trader,* a 344-tonne vessel that stranded here in 1974 when it missed the entrance to Drogheda harbour.

Further south, the Wicklow coast is visually a very similar affair with seemingly-endless stretches of pebble and sandy beaches and the occasional rocky headland.

The dominating force of the east coast, however, is without a doubt the greater Dublin area. Heavily populated and industrialised it's hard to expect anything other than concrete and traffic. Surprisingly, though, Dublin has some of the most beautiful stretches of coast in the country.

There is always the humming and buzzing of the city in the background, the rattling of the DART, and the regular beeping of a car horn or the occasional siren of an ambulance. But apart from that Malahide, Howth, Dalkey and Killiney, to name but a few places, are as beautiful and peaceful as it can get. With the Booterstown Marsh and Bull Island there are even two nature reserves right in the city.

*Opposite: Carlingford Lough and Mourne Mountains, Cooley Peninsula, County Louth Below: Sunrise, Port Strand, County Louth*

**Above**: The Baltray Shipwreck, County Louth
**Oppoite top**: Annagassan Harbour, County Louth
**Opposite bottom**: Dundalk Harbour, County Louth

The Howth Peninsula embraces and dominates the north of Dublin Bay. Its name most likely derives from the Norse '*hoved*' meaning 'head'.

Danish Vikings invaded Howth for the first time in 819 and the descendents of these invaders with names like Hartford, Thunder or Waldron are still alive and well in Howth today.

The peninsula's main attraction is the harbour, which incorporates a busy fishing port and a marina. The harbour was first built in 1818 and was redeveloped and extended in the early 1980s.

Today the east pier is home to the marina and is very popular for a stroll down to the lighthouse where you can enjoy the view over to Ireland's Eye. The west pier hosts a range of fish shops and seals can often be seen here; I assume they're here for the fish and who can blame them. The fish and chips you can get in Howth are superb, I practically live on them every time I visit.

Howth, however, is much more than just a pretty harbour. Up the road from the east pier starts the cliff path that leads once around the peninsula. On the way lie places with such illustrative names like Fox Hole, Piper's Gut, Lion's Head and Hippy Hole. About halfway around, situated on a small promontory, stands Baily Lighthouse guarding the entrance to Dublin Bay.

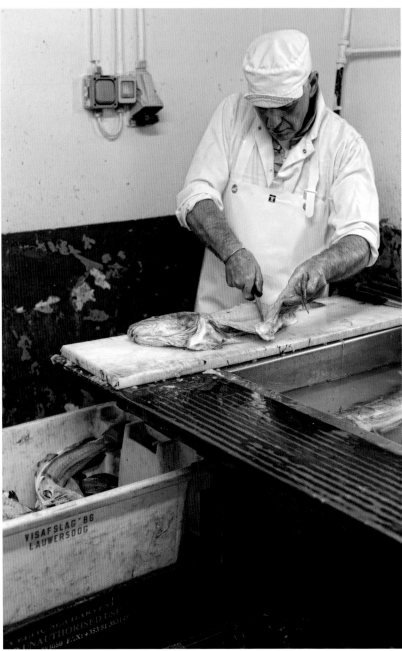

**Above**: *Fishmongers at Doran's, Howth, County Dublin*

**Opposite**: *A Hitchcock moment, gulls at the West Pier, Howth, County Dublin*

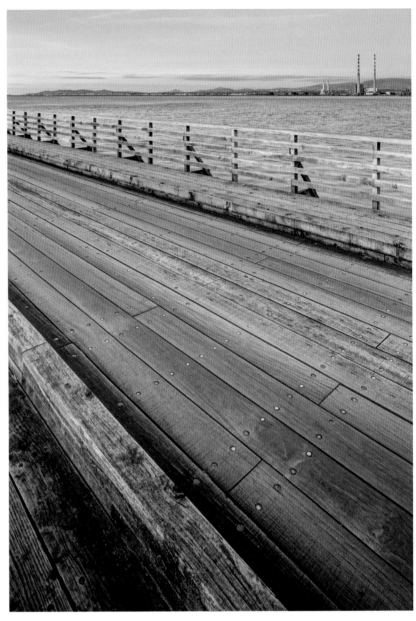

Bull Island is about eight kilometres long and almost a kilometre wide and takes up the northern half of Dublin Bay. North Bull Island is a National Nature Reserve and Bird Sanctuary and holds a wide range of natural habitats like salt marsh, freshwater marsh, dunes and a sandy beach. These habitats support an astonishing variety of flora and fauna. Up to 27,000 birds, mainly waders and wildfowl, are present at any time and the dunes are home to wild flowers, including the beautiful Marsh Orchid and Pyramidal Orchid.

However North Bull Island is not a real natural wonder, it is, at least in parts, man-made. During the eighteenth and nineteenth centuries, works were carried out around Dublin Bay to prevent the silting up of the Liffey channel in the bay and to allow shipping traffic to continue.

The results of these works are known as the Great South Wall (or South Bull Wall) which was the longest sea wall at the time of building, and the North Bull Wall. Sand and silt was now carried out further into the bay and deposited at what, over time, became North Bull Island.

One thing that catches the eye while strolling around North Bull are two chimneys across the bay. These chimneys belong to Poolbeg Power Station, the dominating landmark of the Dublin coast. No matter where you go north and south of Dublin Bay the chimneys are always there and are visible from as far away as Bray Head in County Wicklow. The electricity generating plant was built between 1960 and 1978 and its chimneys remain among the tallest structures in Ireland today.

**Opposite top left**: *Dunes, Bull Island, Dublin*
**Opposite top right**: *The Wooden Bridge, North Bull, Dublin*
**Below**: *Docklands from Clontarf, Dublin*

*Below*: Dublin Bay with Poolbeg Power Station, Sutton, Dublin

*Opposite*: **Bottom left**: *Sheep's Bit, Howth Head, County Dublin*. **Top left**: *Saltmarsh, North Bull Island, Dublin*. **Top Right**: *Pyramidal Orchid, Bull Island, Dublin*. **Bottom right**: *Bladderwrack, Sutton/ Dublin Bay, Dublin*.

**Below** : *Malahide Seafront, County Dublin*

**Above**: *Malahide Strand, County Dublin*

***Above****: Coliemore Harbour and Dalkey Island, County Dublin*

**Below**: *Woman, dog and Shenick's Island, Skerries, County Dublin*

*Above*: Yacht, Dalkey Island and Martello Tower, County Dublin
*Below*: Common Cockle

Martello Towers can be found all around Ireland's coast, but more than half of them were built around Dublin Bay, where all twenty-eight towers were in a line of sight to allow easy communication and provide a tight defense net.

The origins of the Martello Towers go back to the eighteenth century when British warships unsuccessfully attacked Mortella Point in Corsica, which was guarded by a round, thick-walled fortress equipped with several guns pointing seaward. The fortress was eventually captured eventually from land, but the British were so impressed by the concept of the building that they copied it. During the first half of the nineteenth century the British built over a hundred of these towers, fifty of them in Ireland to guard the coast against a French invasion. The invasion, however, never came.

Today many towers have found alternative uses. Some are museums (The James Joyce Museum at Sandycove), some are or have been privately owned (U2's Bono lived at the Bray Martello Tower for a while) or can be rented as a holiday home (the tower at Sutton). Others have been used as a café, a sweet shop and one houses the Genealogical Society of Ireland.

*Below : Killiney Strand, County Dublin*

**Above**: *The Forty Foot, County Dublin*
**Opposite**: *Yachts off Killiney, County Dublin*

Some of the places I have been really looking forward to visit in the greater Dublin area were the baths. Several gentlemen's bathing areas that have been in use for some 250 years can be found all along the coast. They were established as men-only bathing spots so Victorian gentlemen could take a dip in the nip away from prying eyes. The Forty Foot in Dun Laoghaire is probably the best known. The Vico Baths, situated at Killiney Bay, took me the better part of a day to find, its entrance only a small gap in the wall and from there down to the sea. There is something about these places, an aura of bygone days. Although women are allowed to swim there now, one can still occasionally meet a gentleman in his birthday suit. These individuals are, understandably, rather reluctant to be photographed.

*Below* : Bray Seafront, County Wicklow

**Above**: *Leamore Strand, County Wicklow*

## Creative Notes

All images in this book have been made with digital SLR cameras with a vast variety of lenses. Older images have been made with zoom lenses. A few years ago however I switched to prime lenses (many manual focus only), they produce overall better image quality and this back-to-basics approach made photography more fun. Almost all images containing buildings have been made with perspective control lenses ('tilt and shift lenses'), for wildlife photography I was using 2.8/70-200mm, 4/300mm and 4-5.6/70-300mm lenses, on occasion with a 1.4x converter. The cut outs of coastal fauna and flora have been made on location in a field studio. The lens used here was a 2.8/100mm macro lens.

Making the images always starts at home, flipping through maps (or lately a SatMap Active 10), books or searching the internet.

*Great British Marine Animals* (Paul Nayler) was my main identification guide for all coastal underwater wildlife, for birds I used *The Complete Guide to Ireland's Birds* (Eric Dempsey). A vital source of information was *Ireland's Coastline* (Richard Nairn), *Ireland* (Michael Viney) and the classic *The Way that I went* (R. L. Praeger). I also enjoyed several titles from the Cottage Publications (Laurel Cottage Ltd.) series (*Connemara*, *North Antrim*, *Blackrock*, *Dun Laoghaire* and *Dalkey*), these are beautifully-produced books made up from amazing paintings and text on local history. Other books I can wholeheartedly recommend are Tim Robinson's books on the Aran Islands and Connemara, Pat Lavelle's *The Skellig Story*, *Sun Dancing* (Geoffrey Moorhouse) and of course *The Islandman* (Tomás O Criomhtháin).

Although nothing is more enjoyable than flipping through books, these days the world wide web is my major source for planning. Almost everything is out there: information on history, nature, events … you name it. You just shouldn't believe everything you find out there and double check the information you find. The following are websites that I found very helpful and trustworthy:

**The Irish Whale and Dolphin Group:**
www.iwdg.ie

**The Irish Seal Sanctuary:**
www.irishsealsanctuary.ie and www.dinglesanctuary.com

**Dolphin watching on the Shannon:**
www.dolphinwatch.ie

**Whale watching in Co. Cork and Co. Kerry:**
www.whalewatchwestcork.com, www.whalewatchwithcolinbarnes.com
www.marinetours.ie

**Islands:**
http://irishislands.info and www.salteeislands.info

**Copper Coast, County Waterford:**
www.coppercoastgeopark.com

**North East Coast:**
www.northantrim.com and www.strangfordlough.org

**Achill Island:**
www.achilltourism.com

**East Coast:**
www.howthismagic.com and www.skerrieshomepage.com

**Boat building:**
www.tradboats.ie and www.seolsionna.org

**Sailing & regattas:**
www.fastnetsails.com
www.roundstoneregatta.com
http://dlregatta.org

**Surfing:**
www.surfingireland.com and www.bundoransurf.com

**Irish Lighthouses:**
www.cil.ie

**Life boats:**
www.rnli.org.uk

## Acknowledgements:

During the making of this book I received support and help from so many individuals and organizations I honestly don't know where to start. A big '*thank you*' and '*couldn't have done it without you*' go to:

Geoff and Sue from Dolphinwatch Carrigaholt, Mike from Marine Tours, the team at Hook Head Lighthouse, everybody at the IWT, IWDG and the Irish Seal Sanctuary, the team at the Dingle Seal and Wildlife Sanctuary, Christophe and his team at Fastnet Sails, Martin Morrissey of the Shannon Foynes Port Company, Sean Doran and everybody at Doran's in Howth, everybody at the *Seol Sionna* Project, Clay at the Meet Your Neighbours Project, Robert Sparkes at Irish Lights, the team at Conns Cameras, Mike Harding and last but not least Michael, Helen and Emma at The O'Brien Press for pushing me to my creative limits and beyond, and my agent Paul Feldstein.

A special thanks also goes to those who provided me with a home away from home over the years: Christine and James Surgenor (Knockavallen Lodge, County Antrim), Rosemary and Robert Davison (Ballynester House, County Down), Maureen and Tony Reynolds (Comeragh View, County Waterford) and Rachel and Ian Smith (Moan Laur, County Kerry).

My sincere apologies and an extra big 'than you' to the ones I have forgotten to mention.

And finally, a very big 'thank you' goes to Gordon D'Arcy for his wonderful Foreword.

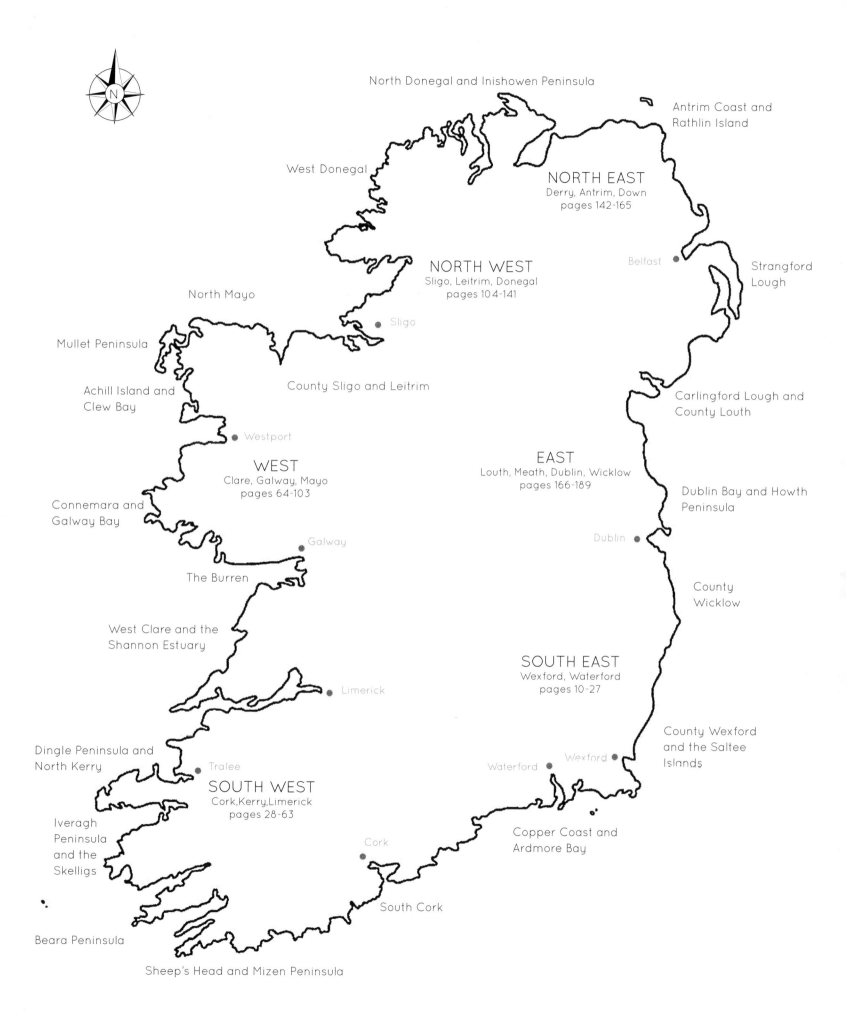

North Donegal and Inishowen Peninsula

Antrim Coast and Rathlin Island

West Donegal

NORTH EAST
Derry, Antrim, Down
pages 142-165

North Mayo

NORTH WEST
Sligo, Leitrim, Donegal
pages 104-141

Belfast

Strangford Lough

Mullet Peninsula

Sligo

Achill Island and Clew Bay

County Sligo and Leitrim

Carlingford Lough and County Louth

Westport

WEST
Clare, Galway, Mayo
pages 64-103

EAST
Louth, Meath, Dublin, Wicklow
pages 166-189

Connemara and Galway Bay

Dublin Bay and Howth Peninsula

Galway

Dublin

The Burren

County Wicklow

West Clare and the Shannon Estuary

Limerick

SOUTH EAST
Wexford, Waterford
pages 10-27

Dingle Peninsula and North Kerry

Tralee

County Wexford and the Saltee Islands

SOUTH WEST
Cork,Kerry,Limerick
pages 28-63

Wexford

Waterford

Iveragh Peninsula and the Skelligs

Copper Coast and Ardmore Bay

Cork

Beara Peninsula

South Cork

Sheep's Head and Mizen Peninsula

First published 2012 by
The O'Brien Press Ltd,
12 Terenure Road East, Rathgar,
Dublin 6, Ireland.
Tel: +353 1 4923333; Fax: +353 1 4922777
E-mail: books@obrien.ie.
Website: www.obrien.ie
ISBN: 978-1-84717-250-1
Text and photographs © copyright Carsten Krieger 2012
Copyright for typesetting, layout, editing, design
© The O'Brien Press Ltd

1 2 3 4 5 6 7 8
12 13 14 15 16

Printed and bound in Poland by Białostockie Zakłady Graficzne S.A.
The paper used in this book is produced using pulp from managed forests